BINGO!

How to Improve Your Odds

Andrew Bowser

Publications International, Ltd.

Andrew Bowser (andrew@bowser.com) is a freelance writer based in Brooklyn, New York. He has been a contributor to *Casino Magazine, Casino Executive, The Gaming Journal,* and, most recently, *Bingo Business,* a highly regarded how-to guide for the successful operation of the game of bingo.

Louis Weber, CEO
Publications International, Ltd.
7373 North Cicero Avenue
Lincolnwood, Illinois 60712

Manufactured in U.S.A.

8 7 6 5 4 3 2 1

ISBN: 0-7853-4927-8

Contents

○ ○ ○ ○ ○

Introduction
Welcome to the World of Bingo 4

Chapter 1
Bingo Basics: What It's All About 8

Chapter 2
Getting Started: How to Play 16

Chapter 3
Play Like a Pro: Beyond the Basics 26

Chapter 4
Beating the Odds: How to Win 43

Chapter 5
Electronic Bingo: Should You Play? 56

Chapter 6
Bingo Goes High-Tech: Play in Your Home 61

Appendix 1
Places to Play Bingo 70

Appendix 2
Find Out More on the Web 77

Welcome to the World of Bingo

Bingo is fun to play, easy to learn, and exciting. For a wager of just a few dollars, bingo enthusiasts can get an evening's entertainment and the chance to win hundreds, thousands, or even a million dollars. This book is your guide to the game, from the basics to the advanced strategies that will help you enjoy the game and come home a winner.

○ ○ ○ ○ ○

From the fluorescent lights of church basements to the glitzy neon glare of Las Vegas, bingo has become one of the most popular types of gambling in the world. People spend billions of dollars every year to enjoy that special thrill they can't get from any other game.

No longer is bingo the sleepy community-hall favorite it was just ten years ago. The popular games are obvious—they are the ones held in large buildings surrounded by a packed parking lot. In any given year, more people visit bingo halls than bowling alleys, movie theaters, or even rock concerts.

And for good reason. Bingo is reasonably priced, long-lasting fun in a truly social atmosphere. In many bingo joints, spending 40 dollars for an evening's entertainment, food and drink included, is already quite extravagant. Compare that to typical casino games: A gambler could blow through 40 bucks in 5 minutes at a one-dollar slot machine—or in about 30 seconds in roulette.

The game has long been part of the social fabric of the United States. Teachers sometimes use bingo games to keep kids from falling asleep in English class. Fast food joints promote themselves with bingo games in which players can win vouchers for free french fries and the like. And let's not forget that Bingo was the name-o of that famous dog in the popular campfire song.

Why Bingo?

Maybe the biggest draw of bingo is the adrenaline rush. Even for seasoned players, a near-win can cause the heart to start beating faster, and yelling "Bingo!" is an exhilarating and triumphant experience—even if the glow lasts only for a minute, and then it's on to the next game.

What's more, bingo halls are a home away from home for many bingo fans who look forward to their weekly or, for some, daily "fix." But getting hooked on bingo is not like getting hooked on slot machines. You still take a chance, but the money doesn't vaporize paychecks and clean out pockets like the slots and blackjack tables can. In fact, many regular bingo players couldn't be bothered with other forms of gambling.

Regular players will tell you the main reason they play is not to win money but simply because it's a fun activity. Casual players are more likely to cite the money as a motivator. Still, the cash prize is becoming more important, especially now that big-money games are more common.

Yet there's one element of the bingo hall that both regular and casual players appreciate: socialization. Whether alone or with friends and relatives, they come to socialize. In fact, many bingo enthusiasts liken the regular crowd to a family. Calling bingo a "social" activity might seem strange to the uninitiated. During the game, players sit silently, deep in concentration, and so intent on their cards that nothing could shake them. But it's what goes on in between games that counts.

One nice thing about many bingos is that you are helping somebody while you are having fun and winning. At charity halls, a portion of the money you put in the game goes to help a school, a church, a community sports team, or some other worthy cause.

In the following pages, you will learn first about the colorful history of the game, what you can expect to win, the basics of how to play, and some common rules of etiquette to guide you through your first trips to the local hall. Next, advanced play is explained, and many of the techniques (and superstitions) that people use when trying to get an edge over the house and their fellow players are presented. Finally, you'll learn about some of the new wrinkles that are sure to make the game even more popular, including electronic bingo and Internet bingo. Don't forget to check out the back of the book, where you will find a list of popular places to play all over the United States, as well as some cool sites to check out on the Web for information, fun and games, and even prizes.

Ready to play? Let's get started!

CHAPTER ONE

Bingo Basics: What It's All About

Since the first bingolike lottery almost 500 years ago, millions of people have discovered the thrill of bingo. Fans come from all walks of life, lured in by the everyday jackpots, the slow-growing progressives, and a newer wrinkle: the high-stakes bingo games that can transform an average person into an instant high roller.

○ ○ ○ ○ ○

The History of Bingo

While bingo became popular in the United States early in the twentieth century, the roots of the game stretch back to the year 1530. That's when a state-run lottery called "*Lo Gioco del Lotto d'Italia*" started in Italy. (Interestingly, even to this day you can still play that lotto every Saturday.) The French picked up lotto in the late 1700s. One version used a playing card with nine columns and three rows, with four free spaces per row.

The caller reached into a bag and picked out wooden chips marked 1 through 90 (1 to 10 for the first column, 11 to 20 for the second, and so forth). The first player to cover one whole row was the winner. These lottery-type bingo games soon became a craze throughout Europe.

Bingo as we know it today was popularized by Edwin S. Lowe, a struggling but enterprising toy salesman from New York. Lowe observed a game called "Beano" at a country carnival in Atlanta, Georgia. The game was called Beano because players used dried beans to mark their cards as the numbers came up. When a player completed a line of numbers, he or she would stop the game by yelling "Beano!," and that player would win a small prize.

Lowe saw that players were captivated by the game. Lowe himself was so spellbound by this new game that he brought it back home and introduced it to his friends. During one game, a lady got so excited by her win that she blurted out "Bingo!" instead of the accepted cry.

And just like that, bingo was born. "Lowe's Bingo" became a sweeping success, and by the mid-1930s, bingo games were popping up all over the country, in part because churches and social clubs quickly realized the fund-raising potential.

Today, 48 states (and more than 100 Native American reservations) offer legal bingo on some scale. Games range

The Bingo King Goes for a Cruise

What can a toy salesman do after he's made a fortune introducing bingo to the world? Yahtzee! Tireless bingo promoter Edwin S. Lowe didn't invent Yahtzee, but he made the acquaintance of a Canadian couple who had. The couple had invented the dice game while onboard their yacht. They wanted Lowe to print up the game so they could distribute it to friends as a gift. According to the trade group Toy Manufacturers of America, Inc., the Canadian couple signed away their rights to the E. S. Lowe Company in exchange for a few copies of a game that would become known to virtually every American. In 1973, The Milton Bradley Company bought the E. S. Lowe Company and, with it, Yahtzee.

from small enough to fit in a church basement to big enough to pack a 1,800-seat hall.

Who Plays Bingo?

Bingo players come from all walks of life. There is no stereotypical bingo player. Most like to socialize, which is why they go to bingo, and they may also enjoy other competitive group activities, such as bowling, that combine fun and friends. Most regular players are over the age of 45, surveys show, but bingo is being discovered by young people every day as a new way to socialize. And both men

BINGO

and women enjoy playing the game, whether by themselves or with a spouse or friend.

The bottom line? Bingo is fun for everyone.

How Much Can You Win?

The usual prize at bingo is cash, from $50 or $100 for a simple bingo at a small hall all the way up to $1 million or more in special high-stakes games on Native American reservations or in casinos. But the prize can also be a car, a trip, or even novelty prizes (in New York, one restaurant gives away margaritas to the lucky winners).

The size of the typical jackpot is based on how much money is coming in. Most halls are required to pay out at least 50 to 60 percent of the money they take in. Likewise, the total money they can give out per game or session is often limited by state or local rules. In Georgia, for instance, halls can't give out more than $1,100 on a single night, though many states are more generous than that. Louisiana, for example, allows $4,500 per session.

A *progressive* jackpot is a prize that keeps growing from game to game until somebody wins it. The house kicks off a progressive game by "seeding the pot" with an attractive amount of money—say $500—instead of simply setting the jackpot as a percentage of card sales. To win the progressive, a player must have an extraordinary win, such as a blackout (covering every space on a bingo card) in only 49 balls. If no one wins, the house chips in extra money to sweeten the pot even more. The jackpot may get bumped up by $100 per game over a number of sessions or weeks.

Sometimes a progressive jackpot gets so big that the bingo hall by law has to cap it, and the prize stays at the same level until somebody wins. In some states, such as Michigan, there is no limit to how much money a player can win in progressive bingo.

Raising the Stakes: The Increasing Popularity of Big-Prize Bingo

The most exciting new phenomenon in the bingo world is the spread of high-stakes games. There are literally dozens of halls scrambling to set up games that promise to pay $50,000, $100,000, or even $1 million to some lucky winner. The jackpots are so high that some hall owners take out insurance policies so they won't go broke!

Some of the super-jackpots are set up to be "step games," where the game pays different amounts depending on how quickly the winner gets a blackout. For example, a blackout in 49 numbers might pay $50,000, while a blackout in only 45 numbers would earn $100,000. Because it's very hard to get a blackout in so few calls, it may be weeks or even months before anybody wins it.

These high-stakes games are found mainly at casinos and Native American bingo halls. Royal River Casino in Flandreau, South Dakota, features a $25,000 and a $100,000 game. Pot O' Gold in Henderson, Nevada, offers a $25,000 game. At Mahoney's Silver Nugget Casino in Las Vegas, the top prize is $500,000, and at the American Legion-Cheyenne, in Cheyenne, Wyoming, the jackpot is $1,000,000.

The super-jackpots are usually winnable during certain sessions. For example, the Thunderbird Entertainment Center in Norman, Oklahoma, has a $100,000 payout game offered six sessions a week—five nights and one afternoon. In order to win this or other super-jackpots, players usually have to get a special pattern within a certain number of calls, and then they may have to play another

Crazy About Bingo?

Edwin S. Lowe, the man responsible for popularizing the modern-day game of bingo, hired a professor of mathematics at Columbia University to create a series of 6,000 cards without ever repeating a number pattern. The aging mathematician, named Carl Leffler, finished the job successfully, but, according to legend, the task was so burdensome that it drove him insane.

game of chance, like spinning a wheel or picking an envelope off a prize board. As you can imagine, the odds of winning are pretty slim, so it may be weeks, months, or years before somebody gets that top prize. Then again, somebody could win it on the first game of the first session on the first day it's offered.

Billions and Billions of Bingos!

More than 1.5 billion games of bingo were played last year, generating more than $2.9 billion in gross wagers.
This year, upward of 60 million people will play bingo at events held by nonprofit and commercial establishments. How does that number compare with the number of people attending other activities? Those 60 million people outnumber the people who will go to the bowling alley, who will attend major-league baseball games, or who will go jogging this year.

Collecting the Cash

Players who hit a big bingo in a super-jackpot don't just walk away with a fat check. First, the bingo balls are collected and sent to an independent testing lab to make sure there has been no tampering, and the insurance company reviews a security videotape. The check is usually cut about

48 hours after the win. If the jackpot is less than $100,000, it may be paid out in a single lump sum, but larger jackpots are usually paid out in the form of yearly payments.

Satellite Bingo

Satellite bingo is another way bingo halls can offer larger jackpots. This is a linked bingo game played simultaneously at bingo halls in a certain area. An outside company links the bingo halls by satellite (hence the name of the game!). The prizes in satellite bingo games are often much larger than what individual halls could offer. Satellite bingo is only found in certain states, such as Washington, where the top prize in evening games is $50,000.

Cow Chip Bingo: Yes, It *Is* What You're Thinking!

One of the strangest variations of bingo involves a cow, a field, and a crowd of cheering people waiting for nature to take its course. In Cow Chip Bingo, a well-fed cow wanders around a giant grid while observers try to guess which square will soon be filled with manure. As you might imagine, Cow Chip Bingo is popular with college students. In fact, it's so popular that several colleges have sponsored fundraisers based on the game.

CHAPTER TWO

Getting Started: How to Play

Knowing the basics is the key to unlocking the excitement of bingo. If you've played before, you may think you already know everything...but how much are you missing? Read on to find out all about playing the game, following bingo "etiquette," and, most important, claiming your win.

○ ○ ○ ○ ○

Bingo is basically a game of chance. Players use cards that feature five columns of five squares each, with every square containing a number (except the middle square, which is designated a "FREE" space). The object is to listen for the numbers that appear on the cards to be called. When one is called, the player marks the square. The first person to complete a predetermined pattern of marked numbers is the winner.

The columns are labeled B, I, N, G, and O. Letters always contain a certain range of numbers, as shown:

Column Letter	Numbers
B	1 to 15
I	16 to 30
N	31 to 45
G	46 to 60
O	61 to 75

The Cards

Bingo players buy cardboard cards or disposable sheets printed with one or more card faces. The type of game cards used varies widely depending on the hall. Some halls still use traditional cardboard "hard cards," or "all-night boards," that can be marked with chips, tokens, or pennies. But most halls today use disposable strips or sheets of paper cards containing a set number of faces, such as six (known as a 6-on) or three (a 3-on).

The process of purchasing cards is called the "buy-in," or, in other words, you pay money up front to buy cards to be used during a specific session. Sometimes the buy-in is for single-face, stand-alone cards, but, more often, the buy-in is for tear-off, disposable sheets of paper containing a number of card faces. Expect to spend anywhere from $1 to $20 for a minimum buy-in.

Name-Calling

Once upon a time, when life was a bit slower and bingo wasn't so competitive, callers would have a little fun renaming the numbers they called. Some small halls continue to use these terms to keep the game interesting and amusing. But, sadly, others may discourage the use of these names in order to avoid confusion and to keep the game going.

Some of the more popular calls are:

Creative Call	Number
Legs Eleven	B-11
Sweet Sixteen	I-16
Two Little Ducks (Quack, Quack)	I-22
Any Way You Call It	O-69

The Caller

A person known as the "caller" picks the numbers from a basket or blower and announces them to the players. It's also the caller's responsibility to announce the pattern of the game before calling the first ball. There are literally dozens of patterns from which to choose, and the pattern call changes from game to game. The two most common patterns are straight-line bingo and coverall, or blackout. (See chapter 3, "Play Like a Pro: Beyond the Basics," for more information on advanced patterns.)

Straight-line bingo. In the simplest version, a player gets "bingo" with a five-number straight line stretching from one end of the card to the other. The line can be vertical, horizontal, or diagonal. The straight line may include the free space, in which case the player would only need to have four numbers called.

Coverall. Also called blackout, coverall is a typical jackpot game. The goal is to cover every number on the card within a certain number of calls. In a 49-number coverall, a coverall must occur within 49 calls, or else the game is over and nobody wins.

The Numbers

The caller selects each ball at random, sometimes from an electrically operated blower machine similar to what's used to call state lotteries, or else from an old-time mechanical or manually operated cage. The blower may have a trap that automatically catches one or more balls at a time while the machine is running. A rush of air blows balls into a chute, then the bingo caller selects the first one and announces the letter/number combination to all of the players.

There are 75 balls in the machine, and each one is printed with a letter from the word "bingo" and a number from 1 to

75. All of the balls are essentially the same size, shape, weight, and balance, so that during the bingo game, each ball has an equal chance of being pulled.

Once a number is called, the ball may be displayed on a closed-circuit television system with monitors around the room. Then, the corresponding light on the big overhead scoreboard is activated. The scoreboard, which may also display a lighted diagram of the pattern in play, is there so players can keep track of numbers already called. Some halls still have an old, nonelectric tote board that serves the same purpose.

Daubers

As each number is called, players scan their cards, and if they have the number, they mark it with a token or a dauber (a special penlike ink stamper). The easiest way to mark a disposable paper card is to use a dauber. Daubers have become an essential tool of the modern bingo player. To use the dauber, players simply remove the cap and press the wide, foam-rubber tip firmly on the square containing the called number, producing a large, round color smudge. The advantages of the dauber are that it's quick, permanent (nobody bumping the table is going to send your chips flying), and easy to see, so you can ignore marked boxes and concentrate on the rest of the card.

What's Your Favorite Color?

For dauber ink, it's purple—that's according to BK Entertainment, a bingo supply company that sells more than 40 billion bingo cards a year. Daubers typically contain 2½ to 4 ounces of ink, which is offered in a variety of colors, including blue, red, green, magenta, teal, and, of course, purple. That's enough colors for a six-pack, which some players in fact do keep with them— one for each game in a session. The trend is now toward bolder, richer colors, such as bright orange. New fast-dry inks are available to keep players from messing up their hands and shirtsleeves. Wondering what to get your favorite bingo aficionado? Dauber four-packs make a thoughtful present!

Winning Bingo

What happens when somebody gets the pattern? The customary way to announce that you've won is simply to yell "bingo!" loud enough for the caller to hear. Once bingo is called, an assistant (sometimes called a *floor walker*) will come to the table right away to verify the bingo. The floor walker will call out the winning numbers for the caller to verify or, in fancier setups, will simply call out an identification number on the card, which the caller punches into a computer that automatically verifies or rejects the bingo. Depending on where you play, the winning bingo card may be posted for the remainder of the night so other players can inspect it. Disputes are not that common—either you bingo or you don't—but when discrepancies pop up, the bingo manager usually has the final say.

If two people call bingo on the same number, the jackpot is split evenly between them. Likewise, if three people call it, the house divides the pot three ways.

The Rules

Since no two bingo halls operate exactly the same way, it's a good idea to read the posted rules thoroughly before the session begins. Be sure to look for special handouts; any extra printed rules for the night supersede what is posted. Here are some common rules you may encounter:

- In most halls, players must be 18 years of age or older.
- Some halls prohibit alcoholic beverages, while others will sell beer along with soft drinks. Outside food and drinks are usually frowned upon, since most establishments want you to buy their hot dogs, chips, and soda.
- During special high-stakes games, management may prohibit players from entering and leaving the hall.
- Reserving specific cards may not be allowed.
- Typically, people are not allowed to sit and watch while friends or relatives play; each seated person may be required to have their own buy-in. Some halls may

require seated players to have an attendance ticket in plain view while they play.

- If a player has bingo, it's up to him or her to stop play before the next number is called by announcing "bingo!" loud enough for the caller to hear. It's important to know that bingo must be claimed on the most-recent number called. If the caller has already started announcing the next ball, it's too late to call bingo. Likewise, as soon as the caller closes the game and drops the balls for the next game, any missed bingos become invalid.

One practical point: Bring a photo ID in case you hit the big one. For large jackpots, players might have to produce a Social Security card as well and fill out earnings and tax reporting forms on the spot. Also, the hall may reserve the right to publicize winners or winning cards.

Cheaters Never Prosper

Whatever you do, don't try to alter a bingo card! It's not worth it, and no experienced bingo manager or caller will fall for it. Many, if not most, halls will be happy to make an example of anyone caught cheating, prosecuting to the full extent of the law.

Etiquette

Bingo players are a friendly lot who will be more than glad to talk you through any bingo problems you might have. But don't forget that you're on their turf. Miss Manners doesn't have much to say about bingo specifically, so here are some tips to follow to avoid stepping on any toes as you make your way through the bingo hall.

Pipe down. The most important of all unwritten rules. You'll notice that regular players pipe down instantly as soon as the caller gets down to business.

Watch out for lucky seats. Some players are very particular about where they sit. If you grab a seat that happens to be a lucky one, you might be asked to move. It's a good idea to go along with the request.

Don't be a parrot. Some people have a habit of repeating numbers as they are called. This might help them concentrate, but it can be very distracting for other players. Try to keep talking and extra noise to an absolute minimum while numbers are being called.

Keep kids quiet. Most people will understand if you have to bring the kids, but they won't tolerate rambunctious youngsters running around and yelling while they are trying to concentrate. Bring an activity or three to keep your children occupied while you play. Sometimes, the hall may offer "fun" bingo cards to keep the kiddies occupied.

Don't take out your frustrations on the caller. Occasionally, players on a losing streak have been known to express their displeasure by yelling "change the caller" or making other derisive or sarcastic comments the caller can hear. Chill out! The caller can't control destiny. If there is a genuine caller problem, try saying, "Louder, please" or "Slow down, please" loudly but politely. If that doesn't work, take the problem to the bingo manager.

Think before you call bingo. Calling bingo stops the flow of the game. If it's a false bingo, regular players might get exasperated with you, particularly if they've already started crumpling up the last game's paper sheets in frustration.

Only smoke in the designated areas. Smoking and bingo are inseparable in the minds of many enthusiasts, and in fact, bingo halls may be the last indoor establishments in America that welcome smokers. But for some players, cigarette smoke can ruin enjoyment of the game or even make them feel sick, especially in a poorly ventilated hall. Try to respect the nonsmoker's space.

CHAPTER THREE

Play Like a Pro: Beyond the Basics

It's time to learn what seasoned professionals already know, from the ins and outs of patterns to the importance of arriving early and staking out the joint. Besides that, it's time to start developing your "mental game."

○ ○ ○ ○ ○

Bingo is really a very simple game. Following are a variety of pointers that will help you get in the groove quickly. The game is steeped in ritual, rules, and special game variations. A first-timer is bound to get bewildered without some sort of guidance. This chapter introduces the variety of patterns you might see, from the simple to the complex.

Pointers for the Aspiring "Bingo Professional"

Arrive early. It's common practice for regular players to arrive at the hall one or two hours before the session begins. This gives them ample time to get their favorite seat, prepare their cards (by fastening them down or predaubing spaces not needed for the pattern), grab a snack, set up their good-luck trinkets, play some pull-tabs, or gossip and play gin rummy with other regulars.

This is also an excellent opportunity to learn more about the best or worst games in town. As you meet people, you'll get to hear war stories and find out about the popular places in town to play bingo. Take what you hear with a grain of salt, though. People might make broad statements about a certain hall just because they went one time and lost. Or they might say, "I love that hall—I won six times!" However, it's wise to also ask that person just how much they have lost there!

Be prepared. Bring tape or a glue stick. Slippery tables can be a pain when you're trying to concentrate on your cards. A roll of adhesive tape should solve that. Like-wise, a glue stick might be a good investment.

Sit close to the caller. The faster you get information, the better. By sitting near the caller, you may be able to sneak a peek at the next ball as it pops out of the chute. This is a totally acceptable practice, so feel free to take advantage of it. However, be aware that you can't call bingo until after the number is announced by the caller.

Stay alert. Stay on your toes, because if you cover the pattern on B-7 but don't yell "bingo" before the next number is called, you lose. For somebody who has spent all night at the tables, it's a personal tragedy to "sleep a bingo." (Somebody who hollers "bingo" after the next number has been called is known as a *sleeper*.)

Keep your wits about you. Some bingo halls serve alcoholic drinks along with the usual assortment of snacks and refreshments. Enjoy in moderation, if that's what you like, but always remember that alcohol can impair your judgment. Don't rely on your bingo judgment to be the best under the influence of alcohol. You don't want to wake up the next morning wondering what happened to that paycheck you just cashed!

Speak up. Don't be afraid to call the caller. If it seems like the caller is whizzing through the numbers, you may be playing too many cards. But the caller could be new, or he or she may simply be tired and hoping to get the game done quickly. If you know you can play six faces comfortably but you're having trouble keeping up, don't be afraid to speak up.

Know the rules. If someone gets a bingo unfairly (for example, they don't call bingo loud enough for the caller to stop the game but they are awarded the pot anyway), citing the rules may mean the difference between you having a chance to win and the game ending right there.

Get some exercise. A lot of people say exercise makes them sharper and better able to concentrate. Exercise also combats the dreaded "seat spread" caused by excessive bingo snack consumption. Be warned, however, that a brisk walk around the parking lot probably won't cut it. Researchers in Victoria, Australia, found that six minutes of aerobic exercise had no effect on how mentally sharp bingo players were compared with their pre-exercise scores.

How to Hone Your Mental Skills

A big surprise to bingo beginners is how often they have to slap their forehead because they missed a chance to fill in a

Do You Suffer From Bingo Brain?

If play leaves you feeling a bit woozy, you may be suffering from "Bingo Brain," an actual condition described by Dr. W. C. Watson in a letter to the *Canadian Medical Association Journal*. According to Dr. Watson, the main symptom of Bingo Brain is a headache—probably caused by exposure to carbon monoxide over many hours in a poorly ventilated, smoke-filled bingo hall.

square on one of their cards. For bingo "professionals," however, missed calls are kept to a minimum thanks to a combination of concentration and mental skills that become second nature from repeated play. Here are a few tips to try out.

Ignore the numbers on the left side of the square. By reading the numbers on the card backward, you may save a little time. For example, if the number called is B-12, scan the right-hand side of the B column for 2's. When you see one, glance to the left for a 1.

Pay attention to the pattern. It can be tricky to keep up with the caller while remembering to check for the pattern. It's not unusual at all for a beginner to get bingo and not realize it, simply because their card is so daubed up that they don't even see the pattern.

Predaub all the squares you don't need. Don't forget that in certain games, many of the spaces don't matter. If the game pattern is picture frame (all the squares along the four edges of the card), try predaubing all the inside numbers to help you mentally block out the rest of the card and concentrate on the important spaces. That can mean a lot of daubing in a 12-card game of little diamond (the four squares immediately up, down, left, and right of the free space), but the slight edge you gain from predaubing might allow you to comfortably track additional sheets. Eventually, as you develop the mental skills that come with repeated play, you may find you don't get any benefit from predaubing. You may be able to simply visualize the pattern as your eyes dart from card to card.

Rely on backup. If you're still having trouble keeping up with complicated patterns, consider bringing a yellow highlighter to mark the daubable spaces.

Learn the Patterns

The number of different patterns that can be called in a bingo game is practically limitless. Most callers know dozens of them. Some patterns are traditional, while others have been introduced more recently. Many are known to players everywhere, and a few are the inventions of creative and passionate bingo players. Experienced bingo players will realize that the same pattern may go by several different names, so that one person's "kite" is another person's "magic wand."

The types of patterns that will be played during a session are usually set ahead of time. Single games are not limited to a single pattern (for example, the caller may call a picture frame on the way to a blackout). It's possible that a player can win two jackpots in the same game by completing both the first and second patterns; or, it's possible the game may feature two different winners if one player gets the picture frame but a second player gets the black-out. Patterns are not limited to one card, either. For example, giant bingo is a straight-line bingo that extends from one card face to another.

Many of the patterns listed below can be designated "crazy," as in crazy snake. That simply means the snake pattern can be pointing any direction on the card. Thus, a T pattern can only be won straight up and down (just the way a capital T is written), but a crazy T can be won on its side or even upside down. Likewise, any pattern designated "the hard way" simply means the free space cannot be used in the winning pattern.

To keep the game interesting, most halls will change the patterns frequently. Some of the patterns can get pretty creative; the biggest problem with this is that trying to find a complex pattern on a dozen cards at once is an acquired skill. If the pattern is complicated, don't worry—it's likely to be printed in a program or displayed on a lighted electronic board overhead, and it certainly will be explained by the caller prior to the game. But that still doesn't make it any easier for an inexperienced player to pick out the pattern when there are blotches all over their card. It's very important that you pay close attention to your cards in complicated games, or else you may reach bingo and not even realize it until it's too late. This happens all the time!

One way to keep things simple is to break down a pattern into its elements. The following pages provide descriptions of popular patterns grouped by similarities. In some cases, you'll find suggestions for how you might think of the patterns in order to simplify things while scanning your cards. Pay attention to special rules (for example, the two lines in double regular bingo need not run parallel to each other).

Straight Lines

In one-line bingo, also called regular bingo, a player simply needs to cover five numbers in a row vertically, horizontally, or diagonally. In two lines, or double regular bingo, the lines do not necessarily need to run the same direction. The same is true for triple regular bingo, where it's possible to win with one horizontal, one vertical, and one diagonal line.

Two Lines

Three Lines

Line Combos

These patterns can be thought of as special configurations of double and triple bingo.

Two horizontal or vertical lines together make up railroad tracks. Asterisk is the two diagonals plus the vertical line down the center; add the horizontal line through the middle for starburst. Bow tie is just four lines: two diagonals, plus a vertical line down each edge.

Railroad Tracks

Asterisk

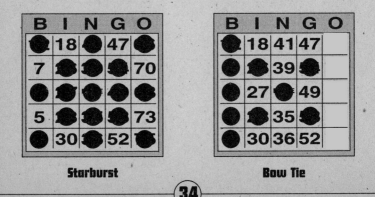

Starburst

Bow Tie

Letter Patterns

Take a look. While this might seem like alphabet soup, it's just more straight-line combos. Remember, if the letter is designated "crazy," the pattern can be formed right-side up, upside down, or lying on either side.

T Pattern

Crazy T

L Pattern

X Pattern

Lucky Seven

Lucky seven is a double bingo consisting of the horizontal line along the top edge of the card plus the diagonal line from top right to bottom left, forming—yes, you guessed it—the number seven.

Lucky Seven

Coverall, Odd-Even, Speedball

Usually, coverall, also known as blackout, is used for a large, progressive jackpot. Players try to daub off all 24 numbered spaces on a card within a specific number of calls. In a 51-number blackout, for example, a player must cover all 24 spaces in 51 calls. If no one accomplishes this, the game ends and the jackpot rolls over. As mentioned earlier, some jurisdictions prohibit progressive jackpots; in that case, coveralls are played until someone hits bingo, regardless of how many balls are called.

In odd-even, a variation of coverall, the caller instructs players to blot out all even (or odd) numbers, and then calls only odd (or even) numbers until someone wins. The caller will usually use the day of the month, a ball drawn from the blower, or some other method to determine whether the game is set at odd or even.

Speedball is a fast-paced version of coverall in which the caller rapidly calls out numbers one after the other until one player covers all spaces. The caller may even omit the letters to make it more challenging.

Coverall

Odd-Even

Picture Frame

A picture frame pattern includes every space along the edge of the card. Broken picture frame is every *other* space along the edge, starting with the corners. An inside frame is a small box inside what would be the larger picture frame area.

Picture Frame

Broken Picture Frame

Inside Frame

Diamond

Little diamond is a four-square pattern that includes the squares immediately to the top, bottom, left, and right of the free space. The points of the eight-square big diamond touch the center square of each side.

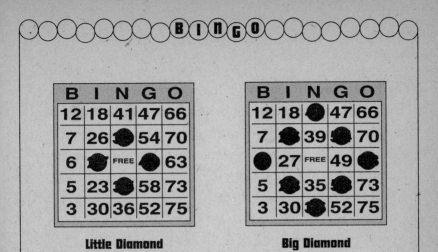

Little Diamond   **Big Diamond**

Postage Stamp/Double Postage Stamp

In a postage stamp pattern, to win you need to cover four squares in a corner. In single postage stamp, players usually need to have the top right corner covered (so the board looks like an envelope that's ready to mail). Double postage stamp can include any two corners.

Postage Stamp   **Double Postage Stamp**

Six-Pack/Block of Eight

These patterns are groupings similar to that of postage stamp. Six-pack is made up of two rows of three squares, just like a six-pack of soda or beer. Make that two rows of four squares each for block of eight. (Block of nine, as one would expect, is three rows of three squares each.)

Six-Pack

Block of Eight

Kite (Magic Wand)/Arrow

These are basically more variations on the postage stamp pattern. Kite is a four-square box in one corner (the kite), plus a diagonal line all the way to the opposite corner (the tail of the kite). A "crazy" kite is one in which the tail points to any of the four corners. Arrow looks a little bit like kite, but it consists of a six-square triangle instead of a four-square box.

Kite

Arrow

American Flag/Castle

American flag and castle are two horizontal bingo variations. American flag covers the top three lines plus a two-square flagpole at the bottom. The flagpole may be on the left or right. A castle covers the bottom two rows of the bingo card, as well as every other square in the middle row. As you can see, this creates the look of turrets on a castle.

American Flag

Castle

Snake

The snake pattern consists of a zigzag line of five squares along the top edge of the card, starting with the second square in the B column. Remember, a crazy snake is the same pattern, but it can start in any of the corners.

Snake

Crazy Snake

CHAPTER FOUR

Beating the Odds: How to Win

Everyone wants to know how they can increase their chances of winning bingo. Many theories abound, ranging from plausible to just plain crazy. There are many ways that bingo players can maximize their chances of winning. This chapter covers everything from true strategies to false hopes.

○ ○ ○ ○ ○

Finding the Best Games

Some games offer higher payouts than others. This is all up to the house, though most states stipulate that bingo halls have to return a certain percentage of the money they make selling cards (usually 50 to 60 percent of it) to the players in the form of prizes. Unfortunately, most halls are not going to tell you what that percentage is! However, some halls might run special promotions featuring higher payouts, or they may advertise big payouts in an attempt to pack the hall.

In particular, commercial and Native American bingo halls may return up to 80 percent of proceeds as jackpots to entice more people to play at their hall. This is somewhat of a double-edged sword, because, although you know the payout will be high, the more players that show up, the worse your chances to win become.

When It Rains, It Pours

There's no predicting luck. At the Gretna Bingo Palace outside of New Orleans, the big game is a progressive jackpot for a coverall of 49 balls or fewer. The jackpot increases $100 per game until the pot reaches $25,000. For the hall to award a progressive jackpot every few months is normal, but 1997 was an unusual year: An amazing 23 progressive jackpot winners walked out the door. One day, a player hit the progressive at 3 P.M., and a second player hit one again at 8 P.M.

The Real Bingo Odds

Calculating odds in bingo is theoretically very simple—it's the number of cards you're playing divided by the total number of cards in play. So if 100 cards are in play, and you have 4 cards, your chances of winning are 4 in 100, or 4 percent. The trick is being able to count how many cards are in play in a game. You can do a head count and multiply that number by what you think is the average number of cards per person, but this can be easier said than done.

However, *these odds don't apply to progressive jackpot games.* Remember that in most progressive games, a winner is not guaranteed. So, the odds of winning a progressive jackpot depend more on the difficulty of covering the pattern in the predetermined number of calls. The odds are so steep in some progressive games that it may be weeks or even months before somebody wins.

Which Numbers Come Up Most Often?

Everyone wants to know: "What's the secret to knowing which balls will come up most often?" The answer is simple. No single ball has a greater chance of appearing in a game than any other ball, provided that the balls are manufactured correctly, that no one is tampering with the balls, and that the blower machine is loaded with a complete set of 75 balls.

Think about it. If you flip a coin three times, it may come up heads twice and tails once. For that extremely small slice of time, it's true that heads is coming up more often. But if you flipped that coin for three hours straight, the laws of probability say that the number of heads and tails counted would be almost identical.

Now, let's suppose that, in a two-hour bingo session, N-31 comes up four times while N-42 is never called. It would appear that everybody who wants to win should collect cards that contain N-31. Hold your horses! Over the course of a dozen sessions, or two dozen sessions, there's not going to be much difference at all between the number of times N-31 is called versus the number of times N-42 is called. It's just a coincidence that one was called more than the other for that short period of time.

So What Can You Do to Win?

It can't hurt to try to tip the mathematical balance in your favor. Read on!

Avoid the Crowds

Since odds depend on the number of cards in play in a game, a poorly attended game can be a rare treat. There's less competition for the jackpot, and, legally, bingo halls have to award the prizes they advertise regardless of how many people show up.

- Play when bad weather or bad timing keeps crowds away.
- Play at off times. If you frequent a hall long enough, you might get a sense for picking the sessions that are quieter than others. Depending on the hall, the quiet

Are Bingo Enthusiasts Mentally Sharper?

Psychologist Dr. Iseli Krauss has discovered that playing bingo is a stimulating and possibly mind-sharpening pastime. Dr. Krauss, who teaches at Clarion University, has studied elderly bingo players who could play dozens of cards at the same time. One woman could play 140 cards simultaneously without making any mistakes!

Compared to bingo beginners, elderly experts had developed a special mental skill for spotting the called numbers and the patterns at the same time. Dr. Krauss found out that the novice player first scans for the number, then looks for the pattern, while seasoned players see the patterns forming as they are daubing the card. That's an important skill to have, since cards in play get so marked up that beginners may not even see that they have bingo.

The results of a memory test given by Dr. Krauss to elderly experts were especially surprising. She gave each of them a sheet of cards and asked them to memorize the numbers in a set amount of time. Then they had to throw the cards away and write all the numbers they could remember on blank cards. Some of the players were able to remember entire cards, down to the very last number. Why? It turns out many players had their own quirky ways of remembering numbers they hated or liked—for example, "of course I would remember I–17—I never win on that number!"

times might be midweek, midafternoon, late-night, or holidays when everyone leaves town or is with their family. The question is, do you really want to go to the 1:00 A.M. bingo just so you'll have a slightly better chance of winning a jackpot? It's possible you'll be surrounded by a bunch of bleary-eyed bingo players who are all hoping the same thing, which means—you guessed it—there goes your edge.

Another possibility to keep in mind is that the attendance for these games may be low because the jackpots aren't great. It would be a good idea to do a little research before you settle on a game.

Play Multiple Cards

The conventional wisdom among bingo players is that you should buy as many cards as you can handle at a time, without breaking the bank. This way, you'll increase your chances to win. Also, as players get better and more experienced, many like to keep the excitement alive and avoid boredom by keeping themselves busy with many cards.

But does playing multiple cards increase your odds of winning? The simple answer is: yes. Say you're 1 of 100 people playing bingo, and everyone has bought 4 cards each. That's 400 cards. Looking around, you sense an

Bingo Around the World

The United States isn't the only place where bingo is played. Variations of the game can be found in countries around the world.

- In India, the game of *tambola*, also known as *housie*, is a favorite pastime at clubs and parties. The *tambola* game card is 27 spaces in three rows: nine columns per row, including five numbers and four "free" spaces.

- In Argentina, a similar game, called bingo lotto, is played in large halls.

- In Germany, BingoLotto—the Environmental Lottery—is drawn on prime-time television, and proceeds are used to fund environmental projects. Prizes include anything from money to cars to vacations.

- Social club bingos that may have hundreds or thousands of players can be found in England, Ireland, and Scotland. Irish folks prefer the quicker and easier straight-line bingos as opposed to pattern games, which they refer to as "American bingo."

opportunity: Buy more cards! So you purchase 20 cards, or 5 times as many cards as anyone else.

Now there are 420 cards in play. In any given game, you have 20 chances out of 420 to win, or about a 4.8 percent chance. The other players each have only 4 chances out of 420 to win, just under 1 percent.

While the math works in your favor in terms of chances, you must be aware that playing multiple cards also gives you the opportunity to lose more money. Remember, you are paying a lot more for a buy-in than the other players.

The fact is, every single card in play in every single game has an equal chance of hitting bingo. There's nothing wrong with playing four or even eight cards, depending on how much money you are willing to risk. A good rule of thumb is to check out how many cards everybody else is playing, and shoot for the average. Then, if adding a few cards makes the game more enjoyable for you, by all means, increase your buy-in for the next game or session. But in the end, don't play more cards than you can comfortably track at one time.

Choosing Nonduplicate Cards

Since no bingo card features any number more than once, every single card has the same odds of winning a game. Some players, however, try to maximize their chances of winning by choosing cards that don't duplicate the numbers they already have on other cards. In choosing cards with different numbers, they are hoping at least one of their cards will feature the number called.

Hold Your Cards Over

Some halls let players retain the same cards from session to session. Is this to your benefit? Well, some players think it may be. They think that playing the same cards over and over will increase their chances of winning. This may be because they have won before with that particular set of cards, or it may be just the opposite: They haven't won yet with that set, and they feel they are "due."

Even if you've won quite a bit with a specific set of cards, you should also consider how many times you *haven't* won while playing that set. If you play more, it's likely you'll rack up more wins—but you'll also probably lose more, and you may be less likely to acknowledge the losses.

Another possible benefit to holding your cards over is that you may become familiar with them, giving you a slight edge when it comes to looking for the numbers.

Stay Alert

You've heard it before, but it bears repeating: Pay attention! If you don't hear the numbers that are called, or if you forget what pattern you are trying to cover, you can't possibly win.

Keep a Positive Attitude

Good things seem to happen to people who don't dwell on the bad. No one knows why. Some people even believe they can will events into happening if they just imagine it often enough. So try having a positive attitude. Why not? The worst that can happen is that you'll enjoy the bingo game more!

Maybe It's Luck

Some people just seem to have all the luck. Every bingo player knows somebody who seems to win all the time, no matter how often they sit down at the tables or how many cards they play. There's no explaining "dumb luck"—something no odds-computing formulas in the world can figure. But even people who have given up trying to understand Lady Luck still court her.

Lucky charms. Statistics show that three out of four people carry good-luck charms, whether they admit it or not. Most students say they perform better on tests when they wear lucky socks, special jewelry, or some other lucky charm. In bingo, judging from the clutter on the tables, one unwritten rule of lucky charms is that they must be prominently displayed during the game. There's no telling what some people deem lucky: troll dolls, four-leaf-clover key chains, dice, gemstones, rabbit's feet, small beanbag animals—you name it, you'll find it on the bingo tables.

Trust Your Instincts

Gold Country Casino in Oroville, California, is located 90 miles north of Sacramento. To bring in the crowds, they offer a super jackpot bingo game with a top prize of $100,000. To win that, players have to get a blackout (or solid diamond, depending on the session), then pick an envelope off a prize board. If the note in the envelope says "Proceed to Next Board," the player proceeds to yet another prize board, where they must guess which of those envelopes contains the big money. One woman got all the way to the third board, grabbed the right envelope, and, at the last minute, changed her mind and picked another. Imagine her disappointment when the casino manager revealed what had happened! You can bet that woman vowed never to go against a hunch again.

Lucky seats. If you're a first-timer at a particular bingo hall, be warned. Once you've chosen a seat and settled in, it's quite possible you may be tapped on the shoulder by an agitated player who's been sitting in that seat every Wednesday night for the past five years. It's a good idea to gracefully give up the chair and try to find your own lucky seat. Obviously, whether a seat is lucky for you or for someone else can't be proved, but it does stand to reason that when a player feels comfortable in their seat,

The Dark Side of Bingo

Bingo is gambling, just as much as video poker, slots, or blackjack. Addiction can lead "bingoholics" to spend money that is needed to pay for food or the electric bill in the hope of hitting that one big payoff. Some warning signs of compulsive gambling include:

- spending large amounts of time gambling
- getting deeper and deeper in debt
- lying to cover up gambling behavior
- experiencing emotional "highs" and "lows"
- forgoing activities with family or friends to gamble
- promising to stop or cut back on gambling but not following through
- hoping for a "big win" to solve financial problems

For more information on gambling problems, call Gamblers Anonymous at 213-386-8789 or visit www.gamblersanonymous.org on the Internet.

they will be able to concentrate and enjoy the game better than if they're squirming around, worrying about bad karma.

Lucky bucks. Is money lucky? Some people carefully place lucky coins in a pattern across the top of their cards. Others would never consider leaving any money on the table, afraid it will curse them with bad luck.

Lucky numbers. Your lucky number may be another bingo player's curse. Who knows? While one player might thank their lucky stars when they get a card showing, say, G-47, another may want to trade it in.

The Winning Edge

If you go to bingo to gamble, you're in the wrong place. The bingo hall maintains a much larger edge over the player than virtually any casino or racetrack. A bingo hall that returns 60 percent of buy-ins as jackpots keeps 40 percent for itself. This fixed mathematical edge over the player guarantees the house will always make a profit. Keep in mind that the worst bet in a gambling casino is a certain kind of bet at the craps table, which carries a house edge near 17 percent. In comparison, bingo carries a house edge of 40 percent—if 60 percent of buy-ins are returned—or, more than *double* the house edge in that bad craps bet!

Remember that when it comes down to it, bingo is a game of chance. If you want to increase your chances to win, look for the big paybacks, find poorly attended games with nice guarantees, choose nonduplicate cards, pull out your lucky charms, and, above all, pay attention and have fun! The social atmosphere and thrill of being one number from a bingo are what bring most people to the halls in the first place, so keep enjoying it.

Electronic Bingo: Should You Play?

Better, faster, more powerful. Is "computers-plus-bingo" a winning combination? With electronic bingo machines, you can keep track of more cards than you thought humanly possible. But before you ditch the paper cards, take a few minutes to learn about this brave new world, which is full of opportunities—and maybe some pitfalls.

○ ○ ○ ○ ○

It's Automatic

C omputers are changing the way we do everything—even playing bingo in bingo halls. In the past few years, more and more bingo enthusiasts have been ditching paper cards. Instead, they are using handheld, portable electronic bingo devices that allow them to play dozens of cards at the same time with a minimum amount of effort. Many players find electronic bingo minders permit them to double, or even triple, the number of cards they can play.

In some halls, as many as 20 percent of players are using these electronic bingo devices.

The best part about handheld bingo devices is that they usually have a tracking mechanism so players will never miss a bingo, even if they are playing dozens of cards. The end result is that novice players can track as many cards as experienced players without a problem. Also, players with physical disabilities might be able to enjoy bingo for the first time using one of these devices.

Players using these devices simply sit at the table, listen for the caller to call the next number, then punch the corresponding keys on the machine. The computer automatically scans the player's bingo cards to see if the player has that number. If one of the cards gets a bingo, it's up to the player to alert the caller by yelling "bingo," and show that he or she has the winning card face.

Many different types of bingo computers exist. Power Player, one of the more advanced systems, features a full-color screen showing up to 12 cards at a time, sound effects, and a small onscreen character (Lil' Champ) who keeps track of the game. Some handheld computers can hold up to 200 cards per game, though certain halls may regulate the number of cards that can be played at one time. Most jurisdictions have a limit (in Texas, for example, no more than 66 card faces per machine are permitted in any single game). This limit probably stems in part from bingo hall owners' fear that traditional card players will stop coming if the players with the machines start winning all the time.

Keno's Not Bingo

Keno is a grid game that is often lumped in (perhaps unfairly) with bingo. Keno has its roots in China, and it was Chinese immigrants who introduced the game to the United States at the end of the 19th century. In the modern electronic keno game, players pick a few numbers (from 1 to 80) on a card and insert that card into a computer, which prints out a ticket showing their chosen numbers. Then, the computer selects numbers at random. Players win prizes based on how many of their picks match the computer selections.

Traditional vs. Electronic

Electronic bingo is controversial. For years, traditional bingo players have enjoyed the ritual of daubing the paper card. They live for the challenge of matching wits with fellow players while keeping pace with the caller. Some think relying on a machine takes the skill out of bingo, reducing it to a contest of who can spend the most money to buy cards.

So who really wins here? Does an electronic bingo player with 66 cards have a greater chance of winning?

As discussed in chapter 4, having more cards gives you a slight edge, but not that much. A player with 200 cards will have an advantage over players with only a dozen cards, but, when 20 other people in the hall also have 200 cards, the advantage is no longer significant. (Besides, players who regularly play 200 cards at once would also have to regularly pay for 200 cards at once, which could have a disastrous effect on the wallet.)

Video Bingo

Another high-tech form of bingo is the video bingo machine, which is similar to a stand-alone video poker or video slot machine. While these machines aren't widespread across the United States, video bingo (also known as electronic bingo) can be a fun, even productive, way for people to pass the time while waiting for traditional bingo games to start.

Each game of video bingo costs at least a quarter but usually no more than a dollar. The payout of these machines is typically 80 to 90 percent. In other words, for every dollar put in, the machine returns 80 to 90 cents in winnings. Prizes run up to $1,000, depending on how much money is wagered. To claim winnings, the player pushes the onscreen "cash out" button, and the machine prints out a ticket that can be redeemed for cash.

What Is Instant Bingo?

Many bingo halls now offer another version of bingo: instant bingo. As the name implies, it is a faster way to chance your luck and follows rules similar to traditional bingo. It differs from traditional bingo in that it comes in the form of a "pull-tab," a small paper card the size of a lottery ticket that has perforated, peel-open tabs concealing numbers, letters, or symbols. If the card contains a winning combination, the player gets one of the prizes printed on the back of the card. The cards, which usually cost 50 cents or a dollar, give players the chance to win hundreds of dollars in just seconds.

Video bingo machines sometimes are linked with machines in other places. Evergreen is one game that is commonly linked to more than one machine. The object in evergreen is to get four corners on an electronic bingo card of the player's choosing (cards can be changed before each round begins). Balls from B-1 to O-75 are randomly picked by the computer and displayed on screen. Players whose card shows the number have three seconds to hit the "Daub" button. If two or more players get four corners at the same time, the pot is split. A large progressive jackpot is available for any player who gets four corners in the first four balls.

CHAPTER SIX

Bingo Goes High-Tech: Play in Your Home

Dot-com this and dot-com that—it seems there's a Web site for just about everything you could possibly imagine. So it stands to reason that bingo for cash and prizes is now available online, providing the perfect excuse to join the Internet age.

○ ○ ○ ○ ○

Bingo on the Web

Attention, bingo enthusiasts! If you're looking for an excuse to jump into the digital age, your time has come. Right now, there are dozens of bingo and bingo-related games on the Internet, available 24 hours a day, 7 days a week. What you'll need is a reasonably recent computer with a modem (a device used to connect your computer to the Internet), Internet access, and a Web-browsing software program.

Online bingo games are a lot like games at real bingo halls, but they come without the smoke and the noise.

The main bingo card is a pop-up window that contains information such as:

- your card faces (usually three)
- the current number and a tote board of previously called numbers
- a list of current players
- a "chat room" where players can type a few quick words to each other between games. To chat during

Online Bingo Lingo

If you play bingo on the Internet, you may be confused by the alphabet soup that spills out of the chat area while the game is taking place. In order to keep up with the break-neck pace of the virtual bingo caller and, more important, in order to socialize, computer bingo players use short-hand for a variety of common expressions. Here's a sampling of the most common abbreviations you'll see online:

73 (or any other number). If a player just needs O–73 to win, he or she may simply type "73" in the chat area, either to let everybody know or hoping for luck.

pls. "Please!" If somebody is close to getting a bingo on a big jackpot, they may type this. If the number they need is I–17, they may write "17 pls."

gl. "Good luck!"

the game, players type into the chat box under their cards and press the 'Enter' key on the keyboard.

Online Extras

There's more to online bingo than the card. Most Web sites that host bingo games include a bunch of fun stuff online, including bingo news, pictures and comments from past winners, news about upcoming special tournaments

---

wtg. "Way to go!" When somebody wins an online bingo, you may see an outpouring of wtg's from the other players.

gj. "Good job!" An alternative to "wtg."

tyvm. "Thank you very much." This is shorthand to show gratitude for the well-wishes of other players.

gg. "Good game." This usually comes from a player who's being a good sport.

brb. "Be right back." Players use "brb" when they get up for a cup of coffee, need to answer the phone, etc.

lol. "Laughing out loud." Since nobody can see you laugh online, players will type this to show they appreciated a joke.

rotfl. "Rolling on the floor, laughing." The joke must have been really funny.

---

and events, and a list of prizes or places where you can redeem gift certificates you win online.

Is the Price Right?

While many of the online games themselves are free, most do come at some price. You'll have to wade through ads plastered next to the game cards or in pop-up windows. Plus, you'll need to pay the monthly fee for Internet access. Die-hard online enthusiasts might even choose to invest in a second phone line so they don't tie up the only line.

Some for-pay online games (which require a virtual buy-in using a credit card or check) promise to award big prizes. This chapter concentrates on the free games that still offer you a chance to win money and prizes. For information about the pay games, see Appendix 2. Also, see "Is It Safe to Play Bingo Online?" (page 68) for some words of caution.

Getting Started

At Bingo.com (www.bingo.com), players compete for prizes in free games. Before you play any game at Bingo.com, however, you have to sign up for a user name. Be sure to supply a valid e-mail address, or you won't be able to claim prizes. Most of the games are straight-line bingo or cover-all. Each player gets three cards per game, which appear in a special pop-up window with the bingo tote board and a chat area (and a lot of advertisements). The pattern players have to match appears in the upper right corner of the bingo window. The Bingo.com computer calls numbers at random. As numbers are called, players "daub" their cards with a click of the mouse. When a player's card matches the pattern, he or she hits the "Bingo" button.

Prizes
While there are some cash prizes at Bingo.com (for example, on Mondays all winners are automatically entered in a drawing for $50 in cash), don't expect the stakes to be too high for most online games. At Bingo.com, most games are worth a set amount of "bingo bucks." A straight-line bingo might be worth 20 bingo bucks. If more than one player wins, they split the bucks. Every 1,000 bingo bucks can be redeemed for a $10 gift certificate.

The winnings for progressive blackout are a lot higher, and can easily top 1,500 bingo bucks, but the odds are no different than they are in the real bingo hall. People can play for days and never even come close to hitting the blackout.

Socializing
If you spend long enough on Internet bingo games, you will start to recognize the user names of certain regulars.

Some games are downright chatty, while others are uncomfortably silent (or peacefully quiet, depending on your perspective). Socializing is not mandatory. You may choose to just sit at your computer and play. If you don't like a particular person's chatter—you may find them to be rude or annoying, perhaps—you can just click on their name and hit the "Ignore" button, and they're history. Also, you can click on the "Private Chat" button to send

Cyber Tips

- If the numbers are coming in fits and starts, you may find it hard to keep up. At Bingo.com and other sites, you can do a quick spot-check by clicking with your mouse on open squares. If a square has been called, it will register as a daub. This is helpful if you want to grab a snack from the fridge or take a phone call during a coverall game.

- Some pay sites, including CyberBingo.com, have an "auto daub" option to bring called numbers to your attention.

- A false bingo (clicking the bingo button at the wrong time) slows down the game on everybody else's computer. Players who have too many false bingos in a day might be penalized.

a confidential message to another player. You may not find that you have a whole lot of time to socialize, however, because the online "caller" (basically just a little box where the current number appears) may churn out several numbers seemingly as fast as you click the mouse. After just a few games, though, it becomes easier to keep up with the caller, and you may find yourself with extra time to surf other bingo games at Web sites like Uproar.com and BingoMania.

Potential Pitfalls

Sometimes online bingo doesn't go as smoothly as it would at the local bingo hall. The card face may not fit on the screen. The game could get terribly slow, depending on your connection speed, the quality of the Internet service provider, the amount of traffic on the Internet, or problems with the Web site itself. A player may get disconnected from a game because of heavy Internet traffic, or because the Web site itself is so busy that it can't handle all the requests. A heavy dose of patience may be required.

Moderation Is Key

All bingo, all the time might sound like a dream—but it's a dream that could easily turn into a nightmare. Easy access to something so fun is a blessing if it adds excitement to your life and helps make a fun hobby more convenient for you. But remember, there's more to life than bingo. If computer bingo starts taking time away from what's really important in your life, like your friends, your family, or your job, it's time to rethink your priorities!

Is It Safe to Play Bingo Online?

Many people are afraid that the Internet is full of hackers who will corrupt their computer or steal their credit card number. But playing bingo on the Web shouldn't be a security risk, as long as you observe some simple rules.

Make sure the site is legit. Some gambling sites are perpetrated by shady characters who, in different circumstances, might try to sell you the Brooklyn Bridge. Other sites are just so disorganized that it's nearly impossible to sort through all the passwords, registration numbers, and Web pages, and if you win a prize, you might not see it for months (if at all) due to disorganized Web masters.

Unfortunately, there's no "Better Business Bureau" that specializes in online bingo, particularly with regard to the sites that want your credit card number to play. There should be no problem at all with the "free" sites offered by the big boys of the Web (Uproar, Excite, Gamesville, Bingo.com). If you have doubts about a for-pay site, see if the proprietors address issues of security and privacy (some post "Privacy Policy" statements or descriptions of the security measures they use). Visit bingo message boards online to see if anyone has reported getting ripped off; the Bingo Bugle Web site (www.bingobugle.com) offers a feedback column where people can report problems with online bingo games. One site, Bingo!@WinnerOnline (www.winneronline.com/bingo), reviews several popular pay-bingo sites.

Don't give out your password. Pick a unique password to protect your account—preferably one that would be difficult for others to guess. If you forget it, don't worry—most sites will give you a hint or the option of receiving the password at a private e-mail address.

Beware of Web sites that promise big money. And certainly don't give out your credit card number! Veteran Internet bingo players can tell horror stories about prizes that never arrived and online accounts that weren't credited on time, if ever.

Look for free games. Try sticking to well-trafficked Web sites that promise fun first and prizes for little or no investment on your part. That way, if they aren't up to snuff, you can simply move on, a little wiser and no poorer.

Places to Play Bingo

There are literally thousands of places to play bingo, from community churches and schools to casinos and Native American mega-halls. The best way to find a bingo is to crack open the yellow pages and look under the listings for "Bingo," "Bingo Halls," and "Halls & Auditoriums." If that doesn't work, try the Bingo Bugle's Local Game Finder at www.bingobugle.com to see if any games are listed in your area. You may also want to check out the bingo search engines on the Internet, which list selected bingo halls by state. Finally, the Aruba Publishing Bingo Directory (www.bingo-directory.com, 888-246-4650) is a travel guide listing more than 7,000 halls, with listings verified every six months. Below is just a sampling of places to play across the United States. It is by no means complete, and it is not a "best" bingo hall listing—it is a sampling of good, well-respected halls. Be sure to call to get the most up-to-date schedules and specials.

NORTHEAST

Mohawk Bingo Palace
412 Route 37
Hogansburg, NY 13655
518-358-2246
800-836-7470

Mohawk caters to regulars in New York and across the border in Canada, featuring regular daily bingo, high-stakes bingo, and video bingo machines in the Crystal Game Room. Semi-regular features include a 7 P.M. "Odd Ball" game on Sunday—bingo on an odd number wins $750, bingo on an even number $500 (packages $25 and $30). Seasonal special events, such as a recent bingo marathon of 50 games including 32 regular games paying $1,000 each (packages $79 and $99). Senior bingo held at 11 A.M. on Tuesday. Braille bingo cards available.

NORTHEAST

Foxwoods Resort Casino
39 Norwich-Westerly Road
Mashantucket, CT 06339
800-PLAY-BIG

Bingo is just part of the mix at Foxwoods, which has five separate casinos, 41 restaurants and shops, and more than 1,400 rooms. When not playing golf or checking out the headline entertainers, guests can play bingo in a large hall, participate in tournaments, or try video bingo. Matinee sessions start at 10:30 A.M., evening sessions at 6:30 P.M. The usual payouts are $300 to $1,199, but there are also payouts of $3,500 to $15,000 in special sessions.

NORTHEAST

Sisters of Notre Dame
50 West Broadway
South Boston, MA 02127
617-268-1912

There are dozens of small, charity bingo games in the greater Boston area, most of which offer nonsmoking rooms or at least smoke-free sections. Sisters of Notre Dame has games on Tuesday nights starting at 7 P.M. For a complete directory of games, call the Massachusetts State Lottery's Charitable Gaming Department at 781-849-5555.

SOUTHEAST

Napoleon Room Bingo Hall
4631 W. Napoleon Ave.
Metairie, LA 70001
504-454-8193

Located just outside New Orleans, Napoleon Room offers daily sessions that include progressive jackpots and "high-roller" speed bingo. Giveaway per session is $4,500, the maximum allowed by law in Louisiana. Buy-in of $10 for daytime speed games and 8 P.M. regular games. The 11 P.M. high-roller game is a $15 buy-in for four cards. Each game has a $1,000 coverall featuring a chance to win a $50,000 progressive jackpot.

SOUTHEAST

Gretna Bingo Palace
1900 Franklin Ave.
Gretna, LA 70053
504-368-4443

One of five major commercial halls in New Orleans, Gretna Bingo is the source of revenue for eight of the Mardi Gras parades that make the Big Easy famous. A total of 27 sessions a week are held, including late-night sessions beginning at 1 A.M.

BINGO

SOUTHEAST

AmVets Post 10
1001 Winterville Road
Athens, GA 30605
706-353-0232

AmVets offers games on Monday, Wednesday, Friday, and Saturday, with doors opening at 6 P.M. and games starting at 7:30 P.M. Giveaways differ each session. More good places to play in Athens are the Elk's Lodge (3045 Atlanta Highway, 706-543-3669, games Sunday at 7 P.M.) and the VFW Club 2872 (835 Sunset Drive, 706-543-5940, games at 7:30 P.M. on Tuesday and Thursday).

SOUTHEAST

Bingo Madness
7139 S. U.S. Highway 1
Port St. Lucie, FL 34952
561-871-7001
877-75BINGO

This is a friendly bingo hall and arcade within driving distance of Orlando, Tampa, Miami, and West Palm Beach. Bingo is offered seven afternoons and seven nights a week. Lightning bingo every afternoon and evening. Payouts of more than $6,000 daily. Daily specials, including Good Neighbor Night (player to the left or right of the winner gets a gift) and King & Queen Night (first single male/female winner receives a prize every time "their" number comes up). New customers get a free dauber courtesy of the Bingo Madness staff.

SOUTHEAST

Unity Center Bingo
2245 Fanning Bridge Road
Fletcher/Mills River, NC 28732
828-891-8700
828-684-3798

This is a typical local nonprofit bingo like hundreds all over the United States. Sessions are on Saturday starting at 6:30 P.M., with cash prizes between $25 and $250. The basic buy-in is $25. Smoke-free environment. Proceeds benefit the projects of Unity Center, a Christian group.

MIDWEST

Oneida Bingo & Casino
2020/2100 Airport Drive
Green Bay, WI 54313
920-497-8118
800-238-4263
http://www.oneidabingoandcasino.net

This northern-Wisconsin high-stakes hall features games daily at 10 A.M. and evenings (6 P.M. weekdays, 5 P.M. weekends). Friday Night Owls session starts at 10 P.M.; Saturday and Sunday Night Owls sessions start at 9 P.M. The hall seats 850 players per session and includes a smoke-free area. The $250,000 "JumbOneida" 47-ball blackout is played every session (jackpot drops to $2,000 in 49 numbers, $1,500 in 50–55 numbers, and $1,000 thereafter). Lucky Seven pays $500 on the same card. Daily progressive games include Bonanza, which features a minimum $10,000 pot. Members of the "Bingo Club" earn points every time they play.

MIDWEST

Big Top Bingo
901 25th Street South
Fargo, ND 58103
701-237-9692

Big Top Bingo proceeds support Fargo's Plains Art Museum. Sessions include brunch, matinee, afternoon, evening, moonlight, and red-eye, with typical blackout jackpots from $500 to $1,800. Evening sessions start with early-bird games at 6:10 P.M.; regular games start at 7 P.M. Stop-and-daub sessions Monday through Thursday from 3:30 P.M. to 6 P.M. (a straight bingo within 10 numbers wins $200).

MIDWEST

India Shrine Bingo
India Shrine Temple
3601 NW 36th St.
Oklahoma City, OK 73112
405-947-3311

Bingo every Thursday at 6 P.M. Mini-games are followed by regular sessions at 7:30 P.M. Proceeds go to the India Temple Transportation Fund (pays for transporting children to Shrine Hospitals). Session packs are $5 and $8; special games are $1 each or three for $2. Progressive jackpots up to $1,199.

MIDWEST

**Thunderbird Bingo &
  Entertainment Center**
15700 E. State Hwy 9
Norman, OK 73026
405-360-9270

Wednesday–Saturday mini-sessions at 6 P.M. (doors open at 5 P.M.) and regular sessions at 7:30 P.M. Sunday mini-session at noon (doors open at 11:30 A.M.) and 1:30 P.M. Sunday evening session at 7:30 P.M. "Mega"-million-dollar satellite game once a night.

NORTHWEST/ALASKA

Big Brothers Big Sisters Bingo
930 N. Monroe
Spokane, WA 99201
509-326-2993

This nonprofit hall offers some of the highest bingo jackpots in the state in 12 sessions (along with speed bingo) held Friday through Sunday. Proceeds support this chapter of Big Brothers Big Sisters, which matches school-age children in Spokane County with volunteer mentors. Pull-tabs and food service available. Free parking.

NORTHWEST/ALASKA

Coeur d'Alene Tribal Bingo/Casino
Hwy 95
Worley, ID 83876
208-686-0248
800-523-2464

Besides boxing and concerts, the Coeur d'Alene Casino hosts $30,000 bingo sessions and more than 400 video pull-tab machines. Free shuttles from Spokane, Washington, 30 minutes away.

NORTHWEST/ALASKA

Shoshone-Bannock Gaming
I-15 Exit 80, Simplot Road
Fort Hall, ID 83203
800-497-4231

One hundred miles from Yellowstone Park, this casino/bingo hall holds regular sessions daily starting around 2:15 P.M. with a buy-in of $20 (varies for specials). Friday and Saturday regular sessions at 7 P.M. with a $20 buy-in. The Saturday Early Bird session starts at 5:30 P.M. ($10 buy-in for 10 games, caller's choice) with extra sheets for $1 each. Sunday Early Bird session at

12:30 P.M. Sunday regular session at 2 P.M. with a $20 buy-in. Tuesday budget session at 7 P.M. with one-half regular pay-out and $10 buy-in. Night Owl sessions (six games for $6) are caller's choice and start at 10:30 P.M.

NORTHWEST/ALASKA

Puyallup Tribe Bingo Palace
2024 East 29th St.
Tacoma, WA 98404
800-876-2464
http://www.puyallupbingo.com/

Daily matinee sessions at 11:30 A.M. ($14 packs pay $400 on winners in regular games), evening sessions at 6:45 P.M., with a warm-up session at 6:15 ($17 packs pay $700 on winners), and late-night sessions at 11 P.M. ($10 packs pay $500). "Royal" packs cost a few dollars more and pay out bigger pots. Featured are eight different progressive jackpot games, including Super Pick 7, which starts at $10,000, and Pick 8, worth $100,000. Special $10 Senior Packs for all regular matinee sessions, and $14 Senior Packs on Monday and Tuesday evening sessions.

NORTHWEST/ALASKA

Tudor Road Bingo Center
3411 E. Tudor Road
Anchorage, AK 99507
907-561-4711
www.tudorbingo.com

This is probably the biggest bingo in Alaska. Evening bingo games, starting at 7:30 P.M., feature buy-ins for $10–$18, with $5,000 in jackpots per session (usually five games). Late-night sessions start at 11:30 P.M., at $10 for a package (four sheets for each game, five games total). Electronic "Power Bingo" units are set to play up to 200 cards in any game (instruction available). Tab Bingo Monday and Tuesday at 7:30 P.M. and 11:30 P.M. with a 50/50 split-the-pot. There is a full-service kitchen, with "floaters" that wait on the bingo tables. Nonsmokers can relax in the glassed-in Rainbow Room or in the "No Puffin" section of the main hall.

SOUTHWEST

San Manuel Indian Bingo & Casino
5797 N. Victoria Ave.
Highland, CA 92346
800-359-2464

San Manuel Bingo claims to have given away more than $1 billion in prizes since 1986, including a few jackpots in the five- and six-digit range. The massive 2,300-seat bingo hall, which has an enclosed non-smoking section, offers sessions daily starting at 6 P.M. on weekdays and 2 P.M. on weekends. Daily specials. On Tuesday, for example, it's Triple Action Bingo with a $25 single buy-in that includes two 6-ons with three payouts for all 15 regular games, with a top payline of $1,500.

SOUTHWEST

SCC Florin Road Bingo
2350 Florin Road
Sacramento, CA 95822
916-422-4646
http://www.scc-bingo.com

Maximum payout of $250 on all games. Evening sessions starting at 6:30 P.M. (doors open at 4 P.M.) Friday through Wednesday (closed Thursday), with late-morning sessions on Wednesday and Sunday and late-night sessions on weekends. The late-night Saturday session is Bullet Bingo, a fast-paced three-number bingo game worth $25 to $250 or the progressive jackpot. The cool Web site lets players submit their own patterns they want to see played in the hall.

SOUTHWEST

Sam's Town Hotel and Gambling Hall
5111 Boulder Highway
Las Vegas, NV 89122
702-456-7777
800-897-8696

Sam's Town, one of at least 18 places to play bingo in Las Vegas, holds 10 paper card/dauber sessions daily on the second floor. The first session starts at 7:30 A.M. and the last at 1 A.M. The Hot Ball progressive jackpot starts at $1,000 and increases with each session until won. Special sessions include second-chance prizes and a 13th bonus game. Coveralls are different at each session.

Bingo on the Web

The Internet is not only a great place to play bingo for fun or prizes—it's also a great place to learn more about the game, buy paraphernalia and good-luck trinkets, and, of course, meet and chat with other bingo fans. Below, you will find some links to get you started in your online bingo trek.

Bingo.com (www.bingo.com) offers a variety of "live" bingo games that can be played in real-time with other Web surfers. Also offers "Planet Bingo Buck" sweepstakes, bingo marathons, and special tournaments for happy hour, lunch hour, and more, depending on the day of the week. Nielsen//NetRatings ranked Bingo.com the "Stickiest Site on the Internet" in July 2000. ("Stickiness" is Internet jargon for how long Web surfers stay at a site.)

Bingo! @ WinnerOnline (www.winneronline.com/bingo). This is an indispensable guide to everything you need to start playing bingo online. They post their own reviews as well as user reviews of dozens of sites, including free games and pay games. Find out the rules of online bingo, where you can find the biggest jackpots, and what free bingo game rates as the favorite of online players. If you have questions about online bingo, check out the message boards, where you can talk with other players.

Bingo Buddies (www.bingobuddies.com) is the home page for a fun bingo program you download to your computer. The object is to play against three computer "Bingo Buddies" and win virtual cash in different venues, starting with the Bingo Buddies Room. Through Bingo Buddies, it's possible to learn some of the basics of money management and odds. For example, while the Buddies play only one card each, you can play up to three cards, if you can afford it, giving you more chances to win. Once your bankroll gets fat enough, you can move on to Church Bingo and compete with up to 60 other players, then Cruise Ship Bingo, and, finally, Las Vegas Bingo.

Bingo Bugle (www.bingobugle.com). This is the online companion to the free monthly *Bingo Bugle* newspaper published in many areas of the United States and Canada. This site offers lots of fun links to click through, including Rumors (bingo news), Astrology (to figure out your lucky days, of course), the Aunt Bingo advice column, and even "Dream Lady," a column written by a dream interpreter. A hot new feature is the Bugle's Ombudsman, a central reporting area for problems with online bingo games. The Local Game Finder, which lists bingos all over North America, is an exceptionally handy feature.

BingoMania (www.bingomania.com) is another free game. To play, you need to download a large program file and install it on your computer. Then you connect to the BingoMania server. The BingoMania "caller" has a clear voice, and the numbers also appear on a big ball in the upper left corner of the screen. According to the posted rules, players get one ticket for every game played and 10 tickets for every win. At the end of the month, 30 cash prizes of $25 are doled out to the players with the most tickets, and 150 random prizes go out to players with at least one ticket. The random prizes include everything from daubers and T-shirts to $5 in credit for BingoMania's for-pay NickelBingo game.

BingoMarker.com (http://www.bingomarker.com/catalog.htm). This is a great source for bingo paraphernalia. Go online to purchase daubers, bags, single and double chair cushions, ticket holders, bingo card clipboards, battery-powered fans, gluesticks, or a red stop sign that says "BINGO" to hold up when you win. Besides the essentials, you'll also find a selection of lucky charms, teddy bears, key chains, mugs, T-shirts, and a "World's Greatest Bingo Player" trophy. Gift certificates are available for that hard-to-please bingo enthusiast.

Bingo Maven (www.bingomaven.com) specializes in gifts and accessories for the bingo player. Besides a large selection of apparel, bingo bags, inks and daubers, mugs, and watches, you will find original Bingo Maven T-shirts ("Will Work for Bingo Cards," "If I don't get to call bingo soon, somebody is going to get hurt!"). Bingo Maven likes to find new and unique products, so drop them a line (e-mail: bingo-maven@prodigy.net) if you have samples of a bingo-related product you'd like to sell online.

BingoSeek.com (www.bingoseek.com) is a bingo search engine that provides some special features, including a Bingo Forum for discussions, bingo stories and poetry, and a free lotto worth $10,000. It also offers a wealth of casino information, and it allows users to submit a link to their own bingo-related sites.

Bingo! The Documentary (www.bingomovie.com). The official Web site of a 90-minute, real-life, unrehearsed movie about the hope, loyalty, and obsession that bingo inspires in people. The cast of off-the-wall characters, real bingo fans from Seattle, New York, Boston, Texas, England, Ireland, Scotland, and the Caribbean, inspired *Simpsons* creator Matt Groening to call it "a surprisingly funny and touching documentary." Contains mature language. The collector's edition of the movie includes *Bingo City*, a short adventure comedy about two grandmothers who escape a New York City retirement home and hitchhike to Texas with dreams of hitting the high-stakes bingo jackpot.

CyberBingo (www.cyberbingo.net), established in 1996, claims to have given away over $4 million in cash prizes. Players can buy from 1 to 24 cards (cost: 25 cents each). More than 70 patterns are in rotation, including familiar ones such as crazy snake and unusual ones such as explosion and slot machine. Every hour, a $1,000 coverall jackpot is offered. While you're playing, you can chat in real time with other bingo players in The Lounge, The Non-Smoking Room, The Loud Crowd room, or even Spanish- and French-language rooms. If you get tired of the voice of Dilbert, the original CyberBingo caller, you can download sound files for a half-dozen different callers, including Roger the game-show host, Happy Holly the kindergarten teacher, Veronica the sultry Las Vegas lounge singer, and Clint the rancher "who enjoys skeet shooting, football, and desert photography."

The Encyclopedia of Bingo Games
(http://www.niagara.com/~rcts/bingogames.html). If you manage to type in the address of this Web page correctly, you'll be taken to a comprehensive listing of bingo patterns, maintained by Canadian bingo enthusiast R. C. Tyler Shepherd. Each pattern, from alien to the letter Z, has a description and a color graphic. Shepherd is very thorough and points out variations found in various halls or regions of the country—like the happy face, which has at least three variations, and the fire hydrant, which is also known as the holy grail.

Lycos Gamesville (www.gamesville.com) is a popular free site that features games such as three-eyed bingo (match the pattern on all three cards), atomic bingo (match the pattern on three cards to win $25,000), easy win coverall (a blackout-style game) and bonus ball bingo (fast play earns more bingo balls). Gamesville has a special "Hyper Bingo" feature that allows visitors to play more than one game at once—just click through the tabs at the bottom of the screen. Your boss is about to come in your office? Click the "PANIC" button, and Gamesville throws up an innocent-looking Web page to cover up the bingo fun until the coast is clear.

What Bingo? (www.whatbingo.com) is a search engine for bingo information. The site includes updated bingo news from Yahoo! and 15 searchable categories of links, including Bingo Directories, Bingo Online, and Bingo Cruises. For each bingo link, Web surfers can click on a button and "Rate it!" from 1 to 10. The site also offers a lot of casino information, and it allows users to submit a link to their own bingo-related sites.